Alto Sax Sheet Music With Lettered Noteheads Book 1

20 Easy Pieces For Beginners

Michael Shaw

Copyright © 2017 Michael Shaw. All rights reserved. Including the right to reproduce this book or portions thereof, in any form. No part of this text may be reproduced in any form without the express written permission of the author.

Music Arrangements. All arrangements in this book by
Michael Shaw Copyright © 2017

ISBN: 1544142307
ISBN-13: 978-1544142302

www.mikesmusicroom.co.uk

Contents

After The Ball	1
Amazing Grace	4
Beautiful Dreamer	6
Camptown Races	8
Caprice	12
Daisy Bell	18
Fur Elise	21
Eine Kleine Nachtmusik	24
Home On The Range	28
Liebestraum	32
Lullabye	36
Michael Row the Boat Ashore	38
My Heart At Thy Sweet Voice	40
Oh Susanna	43
Piano Concerto No 1	46
When The Saints Go Marching In	48
Sonata Pathetique	52
Valse Lente	54
The Yellow Rose Of Texas	58
Trumpet Voluntary	62
About The Author	66

After The Ball

Charles K. Harris

Amazing Grace

John Newton

Beautiful Dreamer

Stephen Collins Foster

Camptown Races

Stephen Collins Foster

Caprice

Paganini

Daisy Bell

Henry Dacre

Fur Elise

Beethoven

Eine Kleine Nachtmusik

Mozart

Alto Sax

2

Sax.

3

Sax.

4

Sax.

Home On The Range

Daniel E. Kelley

Liebestraum

♩=120

Franz Liszt

Lullabye

Brahms

Michael Row The Boat Ashore

Traditional

My Heart At Thy Sweet Voice

Camille Saint-Saëns

Oh Susanna

Traditional

Piano Concerto No.1

Tchaikovsky

When The Saints Go Marching In

♩=160 Traditional

Alto Sax

3
Sax.

5
Sax.

7
Sax.

Sonata No.8 Pathetique

Beethoven

Valse Lente

Leo Delibes

The Yellow Rose Of Texas

♩=160

Traditional

Trumpet Voluntary

Jeremiah Clarke

About the Author

Mike works as a professional musician and keyboard music teacher. Mike has been teaching piano, electronic keyboard and electric organ for over thirty years and as a keyboard player worked in many night clubs and entertainment venues.

Mike has also branched out in to composing music and has written and recorded many new royalty free tracks which are used worldwide in TV, film and internet media applications. Mike is also proud of the fact that many of his students have gone on to be musicians, composers and teachers in their own right.

You can connect with Mike at:

Facebook
facebook.com/keyboardsheetmusic

Soundcloud
soundcloud.com/audiomichaeld

YouTube
youtube.com/user/pianolessonsguru

I hope this book has helped you with your music, if you have received value from it in any way, then please leave a review and encourage like minded musical instrument players around the world to keep playing music.

Thank You
Michael Shaw

Made in the USA
San Bernardino, CA
21 June 2017